Praise for the Book

LindaAnn LoSchiavo's adept, formal verse touches upon what it means to slide between memory, illusion, and reality, at once ensconced in the diurnal and "Apprenticed to the Night." These poems offer us a dream of love that can be actualized with "one's mother reaching out with a father's hand."

Eileen Cleary, author of "2 a.m. with Keats" and publisher,
Lily Poetry Review [USA]

With its title that adapts a famous line by Robert Frost and projects an even grimmer view than he did, "Apprenticed to the Night" is a rich collection, rich in its variety and ingenuity, its depth and insight, and its striking turns of phrase. Taking the speaker from childhood to the present, it integrates a remarkable range of experiences and observations into a unified whole. A sequence of poems chronicling a doomed love affair and its aftermath is alone worth the price of admission. As John Dryden said of Geoffrey Chaucer, another of the poets drawn on in "Apprenticed to the Night," "here is God's plenty."

Michael Palma, poet and translator of Dante's "Divine Comedy" [USA]

LindaAnn LoSchiavo's latest collection is both aesthetically voracious and culturally textured, weaving together family history, personal traumas stemming from girlhood, observations of our dystopian present, and the poetic inheritance that promises to weld us all together.

Mary Sutton, Poetry Editor, West Trade Review [USA]

In "Apprenticed to the Night," LindaAnn LoSchiavo shares dark experiences with the intuitive reader. Drawing the reader in with sharp imagery of night and owl, her lyrical poetry takes the reader on a winding path. Touching on themes of family, love, and abandonment, she pulls the reader from youthful lessons to the ghosts of death's lingering essence. ... Read and be surprised.

Andrea Jones Walker, author "29 Houses: A Moving Journey,"
co-editor Panoplyzine [USA]

Aesthetically complex and yet always accessible, LoSchiavo's collection alchemizes deeply individual memories and experiences with heartfelt universal emotions that resonate and haunt.

Robin Barratt, Editor/Founder, The Poet Magazine [England]

"Apprenticed to the Night" is a full-length collection of poetry that tantalizes the reader with a rousing symphony of language that highlights the full range of emotions that inhabit this collection. From reflections on vulnerability, pain and historical influences, LoSchiavo's poetry engages the reader beyond the page.

A.R. Arthur, E.I.C., Fahmidan Journal/Publishing & Co. and author of "Half Bred" [UK]

LindaAnn is not simply an alchemical poet but also a wondrous storyteller with an almost lyrical style. I applaud her for inviting us into her world in "Apprenticed to the Night" to discover a viewpoint of amazement in the quotidian, the gut-punch reality of loss and hurt, and the heartbroken mirrors of her soul. Sonnets, haibun, tankas, centos, golden shovels, dramatic monologues, and hybrids chart the spiral trajectory of womanhood and growth, and plot the progression of self as it ebbs away from and returns to its roots. A fierce electric current running through her collection kept this reader gasping and turning pages.

Florence-Susanne, E.I.C., Poetry as Promised Magazine [USA]

"Apprenticed to the Night" is a collection of poems that touch on ancestry, childhood, and growth. Each poem tells a unique story, filled with sharp details and clear images, so that as one reads, it is like stepping into a memory.

Cailey Johanna Thiessen and Kiera S. Baron, Last Leaves Magazine [USA]

LindaAnn's latest creative offering is an enrapturing reverie about the human experience--an expert interweaving of lyrical imagery, haunting narratives, resonant emotions, and the mature wisdom of a storyteller who is able to so beautifully preserve both the fleeting firefly magic of daily life as well as its heart-wrenching sorrows.

Clarabelle Miray Fields, Founder and E.I.C., Carmina Magazine [USA]

"Apprenticed to the Night" reads like a table spread for a big family dinner—main dishes, side plates, wine, coffee, newspapers, letters, diaries left unlocked. These themes and characters work together to tell stories of adolescence, family ties, love (delicious!), loss (deeply felt and haunting), and things only done or seen in the dark. This collection reads equally well as a whole and as an afternoon snack. LoSchiavo masterfully weaves old-world myths with real-time occurrences, injecting new feeling into dusty tomes, constructing timeless verses out of fleeting moments. Bon appétit!

Raya P. Morrison, Blood & Bourbon [Canada]

LindaAnn LoSchiavo's "Apprenticed to the Night" tells the story of the need to record and remember that results from the pain of loss experienced at a young age; loss that imprints itself so that a photographic recollection can be conveyed decades later. The memory of that loss makes the narrative voice precise, as if tasked with carrying the truth of every moment forward. These poems chart histories: a woman's life; a family's history over generations; the history of love and loss. All told with the inescapable backdrop of New York City.

Kirk Ramdath, Publisher and Editor, Wax Poetry and Art [Canada]

You may feel while reading LindaAnn LoSchiavo's "Apprenticed to the Night" that you are living her life. The prose of her memories draws you in and you start to wonder if they might be your memories, too, for instance, the mystery of some feckless fathers: "He'll leave for cigarettes and not return..." Her poem "Cento: Benighted Night" beckons "As if the past existed somewhere" — reminding us we can never go back to what was, despite our nostalgic pull to remember and relive. She even manages to give us glimpses of her parents' memories, showing us when a name is mentioned, though the person may be long gone, they are never forgotten.

Rick Lupert, author of "God Wrestler" and proprietor: PoetrySuperHighway.com [USA]

LindaAnn LoSchiavo's "Apprenticed to the Night," while partly a collection of poems that experiment with form, exhibits the care of a poet fully acquainted with the poems written by others. This acquaintance partly comes across in her acknowledging those poets and poems that have inspired her work. At other times, this acquaintance is far more subtle, with the poem "Sticky Figs," for example, composed of ten-syllable lines and including the occasional use of rhyme. Her "Distorted Mirror," on the other hand, contains a conversational voice while using a strong-stress meter. Overall, these poems reveal a poet who has paid a great deal of attention to her craft.

James P. Cooper, Poetry Editor, ChoeofpleirnPress [USA]

This book so eloquently describes the whisper thin veil between our finite human reality and a vast spiritual realm. How LindaAnn manages to capture these infinitesimal moments where we find ourselves connected to an immense unknown 'other' is beyond me. "Apprenticed to the Night" is hugely entertaining and thought provoking.

Dr. Karen Croftcheck, publisher, Oprelle Publications [USA]

"Apprenticed to the Night" begins in a stroller and spirals through life, memories, loss, and death toward a mature understanding of the world and self. Adolescence, kisses, marriage, divorce, death of parents—a whole life unfolds through this poetic labyrinth. Through the spiraling loops of language, poetic craft, images, and themes we revisit moments and people through different perspectives, we see understanding develop and gain insight.

Michael Dickel, E.I.C., The BeZine & author of "Nothing Remembers" [Jerusalem]

Reading LindaAnn LoSchiavo's poetry is like eating chocolate. You can't eat just one; you want to gobble it up. But you force yourself to take one bite, to let the chocolate melt slowly in your mouth, because only then can you taste the depth of flavors and get a sense of satisfaction. LoSchiavo's imagery draws you in and her storytelling is engaging even if you just read through each poem. But force yourself to slow down, allow her words to settle in your brain, and take the time to think about each line.

Linda Gould, E.I.C., White Enso, Author of The Diamond Tree, Japanese Ghost Stories and Kaidankai [Japan]

A fascinating journey from intensely Italian childhood to fully grown New Yorker, with all the ghosts, traumas and relationships of a modern female life; with a similar diversity of poetic styles from prose poem through blank verse to finely structured Petrarchan sonnets.

Robin Helweg-Larsen, Series Editor, Potcake Chapbooks, Sampson Low Ltd. [Bahamas]

APPRENTICED *to the* NIGHT

First published in the UK by UniVerse Press, an imprint of Beacon Books and Media Ltd, Earl Business Centre, Dowry Street, Oldham OL8 2PF UK.

www.universepress.net

ISBN	978-1-915025-77-7	Paperback
ISBN	978-1-915025-78-4	Hardback
ISBN	978-1-915025-93-7	Ebook

Cataloging-in-Publication record for this book is available from the British Library

Cover design by Erin Caldwell

Acknowledgements

I Pizzichilli Ruined Me for Romance—in Italian Americana Journal

Grandpa Umberto's Fig Trees—in Poetry Super Highway, Editor's pick for "Poet of the Week," Sep't 12-18, 2022

The Bones of the Hospital [Le ossa dell' ospedale]—in Please See Me

His Funeral Without Me—in Italian Americana, Dana Gioia's pick for "The Featured Poet," Winter 1997

Stained Lass—in The Cabinet of Heed

Fever Dreams in the Children's Ward—in Fahmidan Journal, "Best of the Net" nominee, 2022

Sticky Figs—in Pennsylvania Literary Journal

Distorted Mirror—in Cerasus Poetry Magazine

The Wizard of Words—in Thimble Literary Magazine

Visiting Gemini—in WildSound Festival, contest winner, July 2015

When Fathers Disappear—in Peregrine Journal

The Bombardier—in Poetry Super Highway, Editor's pick for "Poet of the Week," May 25-31, 2020 [as "How My Father Went Blind"]

The Poltergeists of President Street—in The Other Folk

Emphysema—in the chapbook "Conflicted Excitement," Red Wolf Editions, 2018

The Widow's Missing Necklace—in The British Fantasy Society's Horizons

Invitation to a Kiss—in Pennsylvania Literary Journal

Kinetic Kissing—in the chapbook "Concupiscent Consumption," Red Ferret Press, 2020

Mekong Delta—in PIF

Thunder Polka—in Rollick Magazine

Vespertilio [Bat]—in Italian Americana Journal

Mother on Morphine—in Wax Poetry & Arts, prize-winner; rpt in World's Best Poetry, Volume 1

An Amaryllis for Christmas—in Windhover [as "Anima Agonistes"]

The Grim Reaper as Houseguest—in The British Fantasy Society's Horizons

The Last Visit—in Samjoko Magazine

My Mother's Ghost Dancing—in Choeofpleirn Press

Bio in the Sky—in the chapbook "Conflicted Excitement," Red Wolf Editions, 2018

Cedar Waxwings—in Measure

Embodiment—in The Healing Muse; rpt in The BeZine

Little Towel Thieves—in The Bacon Review

Parting Shot—in Robin Barratt Publishing, Betrayal: A Collection of Poetry and Prose

The Wake—in Red Wolf Journal

Golden Shovel: The Night's Unwilling to Explain—Panoplyzine, as "The Editors' Choice," October 14-20, 2022

Serving on the Grand Jury in New York City—in Pennsylvania Literary Journal

The Subway Pervert—in Indolent Books' What Rough Beast series

Nonet: Subway Panhandlers—in Poetry as Promised

The Bridge Crossing—in Drifting Sands Haibun

Hazards of New Fortune—in Lily Poetry Review

My Dungeon Ghost—in The-504 Magazine

APPRENTICED *to the* NIGHT

LindaAnn LoSchiavo

UniVerse PRESS

We call Night the privation of relish in the appetite for all things.
– St. John of the Cross (1542 – 1591)

Contents

APPRENTICED TO THE NIGHT

"But sweet-tooth Laura spoke in haste: ...
She never tasted such before, ... "

– "Goblin Market" by Christina Rossetti, 1862

A great horned owl inveigled me to talk
About indulging darkness, persuasive
Till I agreed. Is this where wanderlust
Began? A hoot that hints where wildness feeds?

Its sharp beak pierced a pinhole in the sky.
I wriggled in, beyond benighted dark,
Baptized by stardust thick enough to cleanse
The past, reversing terrors, shame that I'm
Forbidden to announce except in dreams.

Outwalking my long shadow outwalked pain
Whose lexicon's imprinted on my brain.

Night's majesty proposed a holiday —
Vacationing from reason, escaping
In midnight's monochrome and cloud forest,
Relieved to be apprenticed to its king,
Always reliant on his entourage,
Recruiting aides for sunless pageantry.

For this I halted time-wasting shut-eye,
Grew feathers, shed discredited panic,
Committed to my new apprenticeship,
Convinced high altitude's superior
To earth, its trash cans, crime, graffiti, grime.

But too soon, temperamental owl withdrew,
Unwilling to comply — unlock the sky —
As if to say, "Not what was meant at all!"

Denied, I questioned why it now refused.
Go ask Rossetti's sweet-tooth Laura if
Removing goblin fruit erased desire.
Ask Aesop's fox if it still pined for grapes.

Its lunar eyes implored me to retrain
My gaze, accept mundanity, enjoy
Scant years allotted to my fading name.

Abandoned by my feathered friend, released
From night's immensity, I watched the dull
Sublunary sphere wink. Hurry sundown!

GOLDEN SHOVEL: NIGHT'S NEMESIS

— *after Sara Teasdale*

Old lullabies hush expertly if nights
Comply, allotting people rest without
Owl-eyed determination not to sleep.

Prayers polish each apology, tired and
Disgusted when insomnia drags days
Into reverse, inventing reasons that
Keep sleep at bay, serenity's foul burn
Pit vast, incessantly replenished like
Dantean images of smoldering
Crypts — restless minds eternally on fire.

Note: Source poem: "Nights without Sleep" by Sara Teasdale [1884-1933].
Note: Opening lines used: "Nights without sleep and days / That burn like smoldering fire,"

CASSANDRA'S CURSE

A tot, still inside a carriage, I
Unwittingly observed a sudden death.
In babytalk, I tried explaining: *truck,*
Boom, bye-bye. Pointing to my doll, I screamed,
"Girl broke." My mother laughed, insisting, "No."

A toddler, fanning grandpa, sickly pale,
I pray while holding his hand, beloved man
I spend each day with who, unlike my Dad,
Enjoys my company. When he goes limp,
Adults escort me out. "Gran needs me now!"
I scream. "He'd rather be alone," they lie.

A teen, adjusting wood Venetian blinds,
To see who's lighting fireworks, I spy guns
Inside a car as sirens suffocate
The peace. "I dated him," I told my Dad.
"Let the cops know!" He hissed, "You're mistaken."

Reality's uprooted, frankensteined
Into a dismal shape, my words transformed,
Cassandra-like, provoking disbelief.

My truths remained green, stuck between my teeth.

THE PAJAMA PARTY

Pajama party! That's what I was *told*.

My tonsillectomy would be performed
In secrecy, as if three-year-old me
Was cast in a mad scientist movie
In outerspace, my tonsils evil orbs
About to be ejected from the craft.

Lab-coated men held something to a face.
A teenage girl collapsed like limbless wind,
Defining dismal actualities
In real time. *Party*?! I planned my escape.

I shrieked — but chemicals mislaid my thoughts,
Eclipsed, colliding in strange galaxies.

Was this an alien abduction dream?
They say in space no one can hear you scream.

Anesthetized, lift-off left me speechless,
Unharmed — though trust, naïveté dislodged.

Suspicion, like a reckless meteor,
Trailed icy finials of new found fright.

Infected tonsils buried, I survived.
But joys I'd once found access to had died.

My parents reappeared to drive me home,
Where ice cream domes, balloons, and toys were meant
To mend, enjoyment lavishly supplied
So I'd forget they lied — their betrayal.

ABOARD S.S. GIUSEPPE VERDI

They sailed, on the Giuseppe Verdi, here,
This unfamiliar country, New York's port,
Unlike the Old World. Many died who caught
Diseases en route, illnesses both feared
And difficult to translate, which increased
Their apprehension. Grandma said she thought
Of Viking biers and coffins gently brought
To rest, those lucky *morti* who had ceased
Discussing coming to America.

Like death's jewels, feathers fell from pelicans.

I PIZZICHILLI RUINED ME FOR ROMANCE

Experiencing *pizzichilli* young —
All Neapolitan adults intent
On giving children sharp affection: kissed
With possibility of pain required —
I learned to squirm, becoming fruit, firm, ripe,
And ready to be pinched on shameless buds
Called cheeks. Italians like operatic
Intensity: emotions leaving marks,
Or kisses raining fierce as cockpit bombs,
Assaults kids try escaping yet endure —
Young hearts confused from then, torn, victimized.

When do I live for opportunities
Like *this*? When do I duck? Always unsure,
Tattooed by *pizzichilli*, mind and soul
Re-enter fate's familiar feast of pain,
Know compromised enjoyment ***must*** be love.

MERLETTO [LACE]

It's noon, a time without the shadows here,
Earth fitting trees to her embrace secure
That she has left no trace, no certainty
Of patterns, leaving our lives in pieces
Near 12 o'clock, day's delicate balance
Suspended, shadowless, conditional.

Reality's removed without patterns
Like shadowplay. A lesson's here perhaps,
I thought when I was four and lacemaking
Took place, full centered in my childhood's loom.

Grandmother, lacemaker, her face worn thin
From secrets, some perpetual, straight-pinned.
Our lady of the leaping fingers, she.
Sly Rumpelstilskin in the fairytale
Never knew slackness of time jerked so tight.

A lesson's here perhaps, I thought at four,
Unschooled, unlike my *nonna*: convent-bred,
Whose hands don't falter though her world gave way
Beneath her tiny feet. She hates it here.
New Yorkers mock outsiders with accents,
And foreign ways. Life snipped all promises
Away along with pretty certainties.

I stand before her, silent, at a loss.
She is my book who sadly lost its place,
Recording everything in foreign words
I've *yet* to learn. Her Naples dialect
Is Virgil's tongue (that her father prized)
Debased — uneasy compromise she made.
"Fit in!" advised her husband. Neither did,
Unnoticed by America's embrace.

I study her. Those movements are trimmed tight
Creating bobbin-lace, diminished light
About to stop her for today, unrest
Instructing *nonna's* face, defacing joy
As she works threads by feel, through memory.

Grandmother, lacemaker: age silvered her
Beyond full-figured hopes except for *mine*.

I want to live on fingertips enclosed
In palms that hoard European know-how.

She shakes from pale silk its unwillingness
To be superior: pure handmade lace.
Imagine what perfection she could coax
From hiding out of *me*? I know we'll be
Cut off — slim shreds of golden day returned
To earth as shadows alter light she needs.

This slender spray of lace she'll leave behind,
Ethereal and printed from no plans
But beauty's memories across pearled seas,
White-capped like virgin brides, their futures laced
With every pretty certainty, those lives
Not ripped asunder. Pinned in place, their lace
(Re-worked for christening gowns), announces news:
Renewal, newborn things, dull safety's brace.

What lesson's here of what I want to be?
Chi son? *Chi son*? My insufficient face
Reveals no trace. Ancestral graces may
Escape my generation. The sun leans
To catch late afternoon. Our living room
Is less familiar when I fold pure lace,
Protecting it from dirt, aware my hands
Discourage courage. No safe certainty
Came looking for *me* at age four except

Low beams of dusk advancing as if dragged
Across a scorned sphere. Twilight blinks. Tired night.
No heart can be heard in winds blowing by.
Like predator or prey, birds nestle in
Among pitch-dripping, tightly laced branches.

Sunset is an illusion, I am told.
Though the sun seems to sink, it's earth that turns,
Impassively, away towards east, a habit.

GRANDPA UMBERTO'S FIG TREES

Italians love their fruited trees — those figs.
Umberto, *nonno mio*, introduced
A gathering young family of this stock
To Brooklyn, pruned, clipped, prayed, devoted days,
Still pinned to memories of older ways,
Refusing to let inconsistency
Impose its stay. Allegiance to black fruit
I learned while earning a privilege to pick
Those soft and sticky *fichi*, synonym
For much not said in front of children then.

Still green, this fig, my oval office when
One's cultivation mattered — so we'd stretch chance,
Obsessed with spreading coffee grounds around,
Massaging the parameters. But still
Bold leaves perpetuated out of spite
Perhaps because life's spelled all wrong, New York
Much harder than in Naples (winter-poor) —
Though rich potentially for those who add
Refuse from kitchens, thick rinds, sour grinds
To foreign roots. It seems some trees are big
Misunderstandings in America,
Its cool completeness not in need of things
Italian. *Nonno mio* struggles, pits
His fading strength against Gravesend's deep weeds,
All dirt familiar. His pipe's a spoon to stir
Blue air, attached to him, one pleasure's home.

This Neapolitan tic: nature holds,
Poured into quarrels too small to contain it.

He prunes. He tries encouraging ripe figs
To form as if he knows, when he's detached
From this, freed trees will do just what they want.

THE RITE OF PUMMAROLA

Autumnal days hummed harvest's serenade.

September's heat surrendered downstairs, cool-
Ness trapped below ground level, drumming up
A breeze occasionally as we toiled,
The cellar, draped in orange light, steam-kissed
By four steel pots at constant boil, rattling,
Air thickening. Delicious tang: pureed
Tomatoes – *pummarola* – slowly stirred.

One table's weighted with machinery,
Ready to chirp with ragtime allegros.

Another's green with garden basil, leaves
Awaiting marble pestle's clang and clash,
While tempting cooks to chew a few before
Its savory aroma breathes its last
Exhale in hot glass bottles' harmony.

Each year, three families assumed a pose
Along the rough assembly line, replayed
Deft movements memorized like favorite
Folk dances. Pot lids clanged like tambourines,
While bottle capping played percussion.

Ten fingers skipping over rhythmic scales,
As bushels of plump San Marzanos turned
To liquid, we smeared paste on reddened cheeks
Of bread, quick guilty bites demanded by
The empty bowl of hunger we indulged.

Our Neapolitan cuisine exacts
Its toll. Traditional delights require
Tomatoes, heat refined, halfway to sauce –
La marinara's smooth red velvet song.

Store-bought convenience was unfamiliar
As hired help or a wax pomodoro.

Thrift and tradition were our household saints.

Stale operatic dramas set aside,
Rehearsing teamwork, aprons equally
Adorned with red confusion, we choired
Tired torsos. Urgent appetites chimed in.

Cooperation tuned our *pummarol'*.

CENTO: BENIGHTED NIGHT

I recoil in my ignorance a little ashamed at my arrogance, my need to return to the past,
As if the past existed somewhere — like an inheritance still waiting to be claimed.

All love, and all hope of love, is a dream of one's mother reaching out with a father's hand.

I'm still alive. My love was tested and passed something like this.

I turn to certain other lessons hard to learn.

Line 1: "Ritorno" by Gianna Patriarca, 2013.
Line 2: "The Litany" by Dana Gioia, 2013.
Line 3: "Italian Genesis" by Michael Collier, February 1976.
Line 4: "South Italy, Remote and Stone" by Richard Hugo, April 1968.
Line 5: "Italian Lessons" by James Merrill, February 1958.

DOMUS PRO CARCERE [HOME AS PRISON]

My kite is cornered. We want to get out
Where treetops wave. But grandpa doesn't want
To fly or talk today. I can't ask why.

"Children are seen, not heard," my mother says,
"So shush!" She starts again in dialect fast,
The funny foreign language mother knows
That I don't understand. Gran won't explain
Because he says *Romano*'s, right, *bene* —
Correct Italian *principesse* speak
In fairytales he tells when I'm in bed,
That I first heard in English. I'm not sure
If they're the same girls who are rescued, freed,
Saved in Italian, like Rapunzella,
Shut up, her rope of blonde left long,
More than a kite's tail. I begged father not
To let them cut my hair. "I can't elope,"
I had explained. "How would my prince get in?"
He laughed at this and made me feel ashamed.

What's happening today? Three blackbirds screeched:
Unlucky sign. I rub my hunchback charm,
Then Grandpa Umberto's crucifix. He
Stares off at something I can't see. Who's *this*?

A stranger with a suit and small black bag
Makes grandma cry. But no one's chasing me,
So maybe it's okay. Our treetops wave.
"*Be*! *Andiamo, nonno*!" I exclaim,
Moving my kite towards him not gripping back.

I wind myself back in, like pulling down
A winded kite. I've lost my ball of string,
I've somehow lost my way. My hair's too short,
Too dark for fairytales. Is this my fault?

Thoughts beat me back like evil birds of prey.
Odd heartbeats flush my ears, drown all my words.

THE BONES OF THE HOSPITAL [LE OSSA DELL' OSPEDALE]

We're making a novena for grandpa.
I stumble on words like leukemia,
Don't understand bone marrow transplanting.

Before my father goes to donate his,
We're having bone soup. "It's nutritious food,"
Explains my mother. But the real reason's
Because we're broke, my classmates like to taunt.

I wonder if physicians will respect
Grandpa if neighbors hate poor foreigners
Like us, whose kitchen windows don't emit
Aromas of expensive T-bone steaks.

Dad's rich in health, the closest match. He sighs,
"*Vado in ospedale*!" Miracles
Depend on faith but don't discriminate.

One time in Stromboli, a ledge gave way —
Eruptions tearing up the crust beneath
His feet — and *nonno* reached out for tree bones,
Dangled all night till rescuers arrived.

Volcanoes are impartial. Which divine
Did Grandpa Joe entrust with destiny?

Disease erupts like blowholes. Lava's kind
To crops — then turns destructive hot-spot god.

Perhaps *le ossa dell' ospedale*
Are saints that guard red wards of surgery,
Restore the safe ground under human feet.

Strong bones of hospitals exist in dreams,
Protecting patients, blocking the cold room
Where promise goes, supplying nourishment.

Dad visits his pop, hopes afire reprised.
Marrow's the monk who's chanting for his rise.

HIS FUNERAL WITHOUT ME

And they assemble, these old men this day,
Prepared for preservation of respect.
Economy of passion scaled correct
For male Americans will be outweighed
By sons of Italy who've come to lay
Il nonno mio to eternal rest.
July air tense with recollections checks
The speed of prayer in Latin's cushioned sway.

Too young for gravesites, I imagine this,
His shadow far too heavy for their praise
To tow where I won't follow. Wind whips up
My want. He can't be gone! Sleep is dismissed,
Distracted. Night turns dangerous, grief glazed,
Fears filed beyond where living souls can touch.

A LITTLE CHOIR GIRL AT PASSIONTIDE

Repent in Lent is what you do, transfixed
On misery, if you're good. I'm bad,
Kick-starting my imagination where
Angelic notes reside pitched higher than
My throat, where a humble alto's swept along
With a choir's gold harmonics, heaven sent
Sounds a family might make if charmed, music
Offering them another heart to eat.

In Brooklyn, spring pushed up loud daffodils.
Crab apples petaled roads as if to show
New marked (or safer) paths. Immaculate
Puffs grazing in the sky became lambs like
Agnus Dei, the sopranos poised for sins —
Peccata mundi — going up against
Determined steel: the organ pipes' lament.

Across the busy avenue, my schoolmate
Agnes is bouncing a ball to litanies
Rhymed, right leg up and under, her dress gay
As Easter eggs although it's Passiontide,
Devoted Tuesdays to the Sorrowful
Five Mysteries. I'm tempted — but no one's
Around to cross me. I'm returning late
From choir practice, rushing my errands
For mother, emptied from soap operas,
Competing with the Stations of the Cross.

That ball's pink, bouncy as my friend, all shorn
Now of our solemn school's drab uniform,
Some gold bit — locket maybe — on her neck,
Hung, swung like a target while she played today,
All unaware of me, my wave, blue eyes
Locked on the ball that's heading for traffic.

Conchshells, dead white, guard her front door, like ours,
Though nothing's the same inside. *Agnes*!
Why couldn't I be known for forgetting?

Sorrow tonight: meal's memory has stemmed
From "Scourging at the Pillar,"
Where Jesus, spotless, guiltless, is then beaten
For others' sins returns me to my oyster
Shell, hard home where I dwell with grains of sand,
Intruders I coat with a glaze to make their
Existence not so scratchy, making it
All easier to slip around till I'm good
And ready for that opening up. From
My curb, I can see over the hill where
A slope rose like a hunch, a humpback whale
Mid-block, fun to sled or bike over if
You dared, no grassy knoll this trellis-topped
Train trench, this urban hillside, its blank broken
Face blocking vehicles, cars gunning for
You with their solid metal presence in your
Immediate future, taking action
That could recast the universe in dark
Unpredictable ways. An oiltruck now
Is speeding, westbound, towards us, windshield coated
With weather, Agnes chasing her ball, bent
Low, smaller, in its path. All open my
Mouth, three notes rising — "God! Lord! Run!" — wired,
Unable to hold words in my mind, my
Prayer brittle as glass. Nothing lived in it,
No rescue, no child. "Your fault!" I can hear
My mother say. "What good are you?" I'm bad,
So useless, and invisible, in shock,
Observing Agnes, on the ground, mouth open,
Like mine, as a red cartoon balloon forms, and
A scream sat in my throat, raw, where I swallow,
Replaying the black revolution she
Took under such a fat front tire, ragdoll

In Easter pastels, virgin-martyr namesake
Saint Agnes slain at 12, an "older woman,"
Mature compared to us. A wave of people
Near her house closes off my view, adults
Who stood around before, all doing nothing,
Gape now for free and drown my sobs with buzzing,
Excited, empty. Two policemen write
On pads as a tall truck driver stands, head
In hands, like Jesus in "The Agony in
The Garden," thinking maybe of her or an
Abyss he glimpsed with no sweet remedy
Of light, azaleas swollen with potential
That Agnes never got to see.   At home,
I'm speechless, normally, a hostage to
The dinners I eat to get rid of them and,
Since Lent is fast and abstinence, there's a
Sad bouquet: pink and purple tentacles
On my plate, curving, curled like weapons, as the
Dream daughter I become makes short cuts, clams
Up, pleading "mouth full!," Latin quiz tomorrow,
And bold strokes I'll unload on Saturday in
Confession as lies. Agnes is with our
Redeemer. If I were good, truly, I'd
Be comforted but I'm not, questions all
Suspended, too mysterious, tight roped
With sorry knowledge and memories ripe
As rotten cheese, my lost friend weaving through me
Like silk who met her dye. At bedtime, it's
A different dark waiting, grave, on-going
Sounds in my mind, truth tied up like a hobo
Sack I could run away with once, my private
Core ripped with wanting, having, not having.

An innocent, dear Agnes, not like those
Kicked early out of Paradise, always poised
For trouble and braced for what's coming at us.

STAINED LASS

Religion classes taught us to behave:
Defer fun's gratification. Submit.

The patriarchy ruled the afterlife —
Along with most improper things. Obliged.
Coerced. Imperfect those Confessions, stained.

Could any child prevent assaults or blab?

Each catechism lesson drilled down deep,
Swore death would be "the best day" of your life.

Meanwhile, your body was a sacrament,
Impure of thought and deed upon command.

Swift holy water dip on the way out.

FEVER DREAMS IN THE CHILDREN'S WARD

"I can't explain myself, I'm afraid, Sir," said Alice, "because I am not myself, you see."
— Alice in Wonderland

Bed-ridden, roller-coastered by fever
Spikes till my tongue choked on uncertainty,
I'm pin-pricked for more samples of my blood.

Depleted by delirium, no cures
In sight, I'm navigating wonderland
Unchartered, watching aides with eyes that won't
Remember them. I've slipped through my own name.

When phantom hands appear, my jaw hinge springs
Open to a warm spoon's curve that's attached
To oatmeal, broth, uncomplicated gruel.

Air smells of pork rinds, plantains, greasy snacks
From cellophane that crackles like popped corn.
When visitors unwrap menageries
Of meat, strait-jacked between sliced buns,
My mouth starts watering. This long malaise
Undressed me of fat, strength. If Death inched in,
Could I caterpillar myself away?

> That rabbit's back, white masked, and furrowing
> In haste as twilight iced the windowsills.
> Berating me because of my drab gown,
> It peels fruit, dresses me in honeyed rinds,
> Adorns my unwashed hair with sheets of mist.
> Mad Hatter looks annoyed, presiding like
> A garden god, when I request sliced cake.
> "Cottontail has your cure," swore Jabberwock.
> A sign read, "Taste me!" Its glass door was locked.
> All alabaster splendor, rabbit ran

Past, his red tie becoming roses dead
From disregard, resigned to cold, hard dirt.
White Queen shrieked, "Child! Don't lose your head!"
World waits.

Intruder fever slips away, shh, shh.
My spirit claps, "Bring me some real food, please!"

STICKY FIGS

The Italians vulgarly say, it stands for the female part; the fig-fruit:
The fissure, the yoni,
The wonderful moist conductivity towards the centre. …
"Figs" by D.H. Lawrence, 1924

Before I'm old enough to be some boy's
Intense, low-calorie, half innocent
Lip-smacking snack that leaves his young mouth wet
With decadent tastes, cravings that rock him
Awake, I learned to test a milky-sapped
Sac on its stem. Until it's ripe, you can't
Disturb a fig. Don't suck it, cradling
Its tender wrapper of unripened skin.

All winter, fig trees huddle under tarps,
Enjoying long pajama parties, stark
Naked, their branches tied, unable to stretch.

This hibernation — their adolescence —
Creates desired sweetness through its stem.

In autumn dried fruit decorates the plates,
Bright, wrinkled apricots, dark juicy figs,
Patience rewarded. With maturity
Comes knowing when to loot the tree — or wait.

DISTORTED MIRROR

Because the other girls wore push-up bras
And Sweetie didn't, I got curious.
Instead of wearing low-cut denims that
Revealed a lacy thong, she chose full skirts.

Once in the cafeteria I ate
Too much and Sweetie demonstrated all
The various creative ways to purge,
Held my hair. "Better?" she asked. *OMG*!

That's how our friendship started — on empty.

"We're besties now!" I told my mother but
Omitting how those toothbrush tactics helped
Dislodge food. How we gorged on ice cream, cakes,
Pies, vomited together, side by side,
Like goddesses with sacred rituals,
Rewarded with a flatter stomach. Then
Snug pants seemed looser. Hipbones strutted out.

Eventually, toilets taunted me,
Bare tiles too painful for my bony knees.
I wore more layers, hid under wide skirts.

The male gaze, saturated sex and smirk,
Avoided us. Females were envious.

Soon Sweetie and I grew competitive.
Who could stop menstruating first? Who would
Lose more weight? She discovered laxatives,
Bragging that her commitment was total.

I fasted till I couldn't concentrate
In class, made lame excuses, anything
That might distract my teachers or buy time.

My weight caused incoherence. Friends weighed in,
Deciding who looked better, prettier,
More "runway fashion model" look-alike.
Few classmates voted for me. Sweetie won.

Physicians never spoke in English, used
Expressions they made up: "bulimia,"
"Body dysmorphia," "anorexic."

My Dad said "self-destructive." But my Mom,
Always dramatic, called it "a death wish."

This incoherence chewed me up, spat out
Illogical opinions, sickening,
Unhealthy, empty calorie theories
That only caused confusion and alarm.

Even before the toothbrush-toilet-thing
With Sweetie, honesty patrolled my room.

The moon-eyed courtyard of my cheval glass
Reflected on this, winked at me: "*You're **fat**!*"

GOLDEN SHOVEL: TENEBRIFIC

— after Neal Bowers

When I was ten, he forgot me at the butcher, inevitably care-
less.

I met strangers' eyes with the rapture of recognition, whether
man
or teenager, until proven wrong. Eventually, a policeman took
my
hand, cradling our soup bones with unremitting care — like a
father
in training. Afterwards, the stench of bloody sawdust always
reminded me of abandonment. I ate less and less, leaving
my meals and my solidity behind, slowly becoming a ghost. The
me
who was ten years old grew another self who appeared at
will, an impostor rehearsing departure, thumbing rides at bus-
stops or rest-stops.

Note: Source poem: "Tenth-Year Elegy" by Neal Bowers, 1990.
Note: Opening lines used: "Careless man, my father, / always leaving me at rest-stops,"

THE WIZARD OF WORDS

The gift of narrative my father had.
Conflict became adventure in his hands.
His penitentiary of poverty
During the Great Depression was reformed
Through humorous accounts that made us sad
We weren't born yet, rationed for after.

In the uneasy partnership of two
Tongues, English and Italian, he trimmed lines
To master his material. Threads were
Slight that tied him to joy but using text
He wove strong clothing that protected him.

Instructions were unwrapped in the produce
Department of a store when customers
Demanded better fruit. He pared away
The bad parts and in this, too, he learned more
About great storytelling: minimize,
Select. Though later narratives would be
Composed by losses and bad choices, his
Telling restored weight to its proper place,
His words at dinnertime kept holding us
Through sunsets in a fiery embrace.

VISITING GEMINI

Sitting we wait for M-G-M Grand Air.
Sunglassed, that one's my father — but he's grown
A twin. One man gave me piggyback rides, named
Great stars in heaven, christened strange dustballs
Under my bed, making light of the dark,
Hugger called "dear Dadds," even when he left,
Went West to write. But shading reptile eyes:
Another guy my Mom's warned me about,
Who swears by bio-rhythms while angling
Development deals, praises re-hab groups.
"Poor women preyed on!" sniffs my aunt — pray *with*
Perhaps, since his hugs have gotten thinner.

Here his "Whaddya want?" means for dinner.

What I want is to skip again, a hand
On either side. I'm tired of riots,
Goat cheese on food, not knowing who's used a bed.
His old apartment's nicer. Here police
Cruise in "a black and normal" and his friends
Seem so wild. Why is Angel skinny (if
Not "on meth" anymore)? There's Beth who needs
White mice because she keeps this snake. Dear Dadds
Must think he's Bogey: all I hear is "kid."
— "What's her sign?" — "Virgo, aren't you, kid?" What is
A grown-up doing with a python? It's
Called Gemini. Who cares if Cher's across
Our table? Tell me: what *is* that? I care about
This writer with no paper in his house,
No ribbons, stamps — then empties block his deck!

I wish he'd point at Pegasus's neck
Without that smell on his breath. ***DADDS***! *Suggest*
We ***BOTH*** *walk through that gate*! No. His goodbye —
With shades on — is: "Don't mention Gemini."

WHEN FATHERS DISAPPEAR

When fathers disappear, they take their name —
Along with the certainty they loved those who
Were left behind, deserted. Families
Can overwinter, silent, wondering.

Perhaps his name was fake, an alias.

Deceptive Dad erase all memories:
Cold righteous looks, prophetic sighs, door slams.
He'd been a mouthpiece, a provider once.

Imaginative words, incisive wit
Will introduce himself to women's eyes,
Who'll see potential, dream's aristocrat,
Misreading his moods for profundity.

All unaware, one blindly takes him in.

Compliance has its price, which makes him twitch,
Then adumbrate new plans each time he shaves.

When gearshifts of a train have more appeal
Than bottomless parental collar-grabs,
He'll leave for cigarettes and not return —
Nor face those bad names touching everything.

THE BOMBARDIER

My father slowly lost his vision though
He didn't see it coming. His teenage
Face, tilting upwards, studied Brooklyn's sky
On Independence Day. Bright flashes flung
Towards heaven — Roman candles, comets — spoke
In German: mortars, aerial shells, mines.

His family watched as Hitler hogged headlines:
Annihilation, concentration camps.

When Uncle Sam knocked, he surrendered thick
Italian hair, mock manhood's pompadour.

Unlike shorn Samson, he felt stronger, believed
That if G.I.s hoped, fought for victory,
The universe would pay attention, might
Mold wanting into bold reality.

His twenty-twenty was not good enough
For flight school — only adequate to gain
Eligibility to jump from planes.

The bomb squad stayed intact, forever friends,
Fired off missives, air-mailed, unafraid,
Creating camaraderie tighter
Than elbow room inside their Air Force plane.

Survival, faith, salvation strengthened them.
The baby boom rewarded bravery,
Peace spinning into gold reality.

Their pilot went blind first, his vision peeled
Away like sunburnt skin. But Uncle Sam
Disavowed all responsibility
As, one by one, they lost the gift of sight.

The universe stopped paying attention here.

My father's retinas released their grasp
Of greens and grays. He couldn't drive at night.
Newspapers' small fonts became unreadable.

Small drusen — stoney granules — multiplied.

He dreamt of black-outs, Europe occupied.
He couldn't sketch the faces of fallen friends,
Lost his ability to tell claret
Apart from a Chianti Classico,
Detect a weed from grapevines, watch sunset.

Now blindness held him in captivity.

When death escorted him to quieter
Corridors, his eyes up-turned, all prepared
To face the fusillade of so much light.

THE POLTERGEISTS OF PRESIDENT STREET

The memory knocks insistently, rattles its chain. The story retold, summoned, shared like leftovers from a phantom feast. My uncle's voice, an incantation that wiped the table clean of holiday food, poured the chill down the backs of our collars, goosefleshed our arms, as he explained how most ghosts are a disappearing act, but poltergeists engineer noisy return engagements. Vaudevillians of the void, greedy for a live audience.

A lifetime ago, his weekly poker game was dinner-theatre for restless spirits stuck in a haunted house. He carried in his gut hunger boxed inside the Great Depression, festering impatience, unquiet cravings. Nicotine nursed him daily, except when he donned altar-boy drag: cassock and surplice. The priest would elevate the host to an invisible God, his thurible filling the air with holy smoke. "Saints have no opportunity to stay dead," he thought, cupping a fist to the flame, inhaling an unfiltered Lucky Strike behind the rectory as his eyes scanned his surroundings and a "Room for Rent" drifted into view.

Complaints had carved an abyss between himself and his parents. They were inhospitable to the stink of stogies and cigarettes that fueled rounds of poker, angling their eyes like a crucified Christ, imploring the card players to quit. He needed a new venue, and offering rent money was his ace.

He ran enthusiastically up the stoop as a wan housewife ghosted into view, her face wreathed by a French inhale. A deal was struck for two games during weeknights, eight in a month, paid in advance. From an inner sanctum, a room he could not see, an unearthly falsetto shrieked, dimming the sunshine, roaring into his ears.

"We have ghosts," she explained. "No extra charge."

Now those long-ago scares rose like steam, in the same way a flayed turkey breast releases its heat to the carving knife. Then came not the rapping, tapping Poe heard on his chamber door but the crashing, smashing of crockery shelved in china cabinets, glassware thrown at the stove, forcing the players to their feet, hunting for the source of the commotion, only to find nothing. To my uncle's eye, though, there were no cabinets—at least, not anymore. There had been, at one time, but the furious being continued smashing them, in their absence, decades later.

On other evenings, spooks would overturn the table, sending hearts and clubs airborne, alarming all. Haunting memories must have gnawed at the apparition's loneliness, continuing a ferocious domestic drama, echoing long ago chaos.

Priests came and went, their blessings, novenas, incense, prayers brittle as glass. Nothing lived in these invocations: no exorcism, no catharsis.

Collectively, our blood forgets to surge and flow as we shiver on the brink of climax. My uncle's closing act, ventriloquy, fills the room with unhinged cackling, a poltergeist maniacally gleeful. Proud of its performance as our soup pot boils dry and our percolator shrieks.

Years after, I dream of what must have happened to wind a spirit so angrily to that house: a slow-cooked rage, the soughing wind taunting the drawn shades, tattered scullery wallpaper scuffed by body slams. A furious spouse. Abuse accumulated, stoking a fire in the belly. Well-oiled revenge readying, seething, sharpening a six-inch boning knife. A marital ragout splattered across the wall. Now a dirge lullabies her ears as she swoons around the house, searching for a shovel, lozenging the word burial under her tongue. She begins her maniacal laughter.

Tomorrow's empty jar of morning fills with men in white coats and a restraining garment nearly split open by wild whoops of merriment, freedom from her husband's rage. At last there's a sense of the future humming.

Except it would not end there. Emotions drowned in this bloody kitchen would resurface, be regurgitated. Have the last laugh.

EMPHYSEMA

My uncle coughed through every call. I wished
He'd want to live not choke, not smoke, pushed through
To past tense, with his fast life done, run like
Butter through fingers, rich once, then all gone.

Negotiating, I would fight for words.

He'd find forgetfulness in nicotine,
Thick phlegm like time's raccoon impatiently
Poised, waiting with its sharp claws and greedy jaw.

Already I see red around each gasp.
Thin mucous spits the air like pissed-off ghosts.

Cold comes between us — dread hands closing in.

THE WIDOW'S MISSING NECKLACE

He promised everything, in time, improves.
If wedlock's root is trust, is love removed
By death? His widow finds it hard to sleep
Alone. Bereavement's hollowed her pale cheeks,
Uncaressed. Robbed of joy, her spirit's bruised.

An anniversary gift, precious jewels,
Cannot be found. This necklace was not moved
Nor worn since he fell ill. Again she weeps.
He promised everything.

Ghost husband, undetected, jangled loose
Her precious pearls, its faulty catch fine-tuned.
Repairing jewelry does not come cheap —
Despite the fact this goldsmith was deceased.
He buried it in bedding, feeling shrewd.
My aunt thinks spooks exist. This can't be proved.
He promised everything.

Note: On the first anniversary of his death, my uncle returned the missing necklace to his widow. The faulty clasp had been repaired.

GOLDEN SHOVEL: AT NIGHT ALONE

– after Sara Teasdale

Enchanted by sly sunless streetscapes, I
Explored my city fearlessly and went
To precincts strange, unknown, and silent out
Of curiosity, enraptured at
Imaginary fireflies lighting night
On my behalf, protecting me. Alone,
My sole companions shadows, hours fooled the
Clock who resigned imperious rule. My young
Unruly nature gave permission. Blood
Obeyed when impulsiveness was flowing.

Note: Source poem: "Winter Stars" by Sara Teasdale [1884 — 1933], 1920.
Note: Opening lines used: "I went out at night alone; / The young blood flowing"

IMPATIENS BUDDING

What keeps us up? Your friendship's all I have —
Riches I couldn't be extravagant
With, spiritual broth concocted, stirred
Long years ago, left undiluted. I'd
Be running, empty; your blue eyes refueled
Me through the peace of simply being there.
Between us, even harmless things absorbed
Raw energy and meaning, buoyed us up.

What's happening today? Our picnic rained
Us in. Your blanket on the floor, we faced
Glass garden doors. Through passion of the storm,
I saw a plant I'd given you that time
You struggled with a fever, lay bed-bound.

It's grown — that red impatiens balsamina,
Nicknamed the "Touch-Me-Not" — forgotten now
And pelted by surprising downfalls. "I'll
Go rescue it!" I say, aware you've just
Been eyeing up my legs, inclined towards me
In all new ways. I don't know what to say.

Am I imagining this? Underneath
My naked legs, this fabric touches off
Unnameable anxieties of you
In bed too ill to do the simple things
That I dropped by to do for helpless you,
Two trapped by passion of uncertainty
Back then — perhaps again fond victims touched,
Arresting fever, guarded, wondering
As tight impatiens buds are poised for first
Direction, naturally inclined (though still
Unseeing) towards heat's light. That storm keeps up.

New buds stay down. For you, old friend, I hold
Aloft the peace of all I won't deny.

Today we're watchful apple pickers rained
Out of the garden. Not for us. Not yet.

INVITATION TO A KISS

Some kisses are consumer errors. You'd
Try taking them back if you could. I'm hooked
On kisses warming me like cognac, poured
On my lips, heat transferring. I expect
Machines pre-loaded with kiss silver; I
Might gamble — costumed as the Queen of Hearts.

So far, I've never been caught or blackballed
For cheating during kissing, though I'm known
To leave a kissing booth without payment.

A certain kiss is on my bucket list:
That kiss-as-condor, breathlessly sublime,
Transporting me, eyes closed, flown secretly
To boundless kingdoms with a pleasure dome,
Watched over by one dedicated tree
Lodged in the dimple of a distant peak,
Its splendor as a sign I was there — once.

KINETIC KISSING

I've never grown accustomed to the pause
Between sharp lightning and its boom, the rift
Between the accidental kiss that slipped
Between my lips instead of grazing skin.

Awaiting night's approach, I can't predict
How far it might go, how it twists, explodes.
But science can't touch the ineffable.
Emotions can be indefinable.

Electric bolts and booms confuse wildlife.
Calamity does not charm animals.
Protective instinct guides them straight away.

But sudden interruption from dull life —
Dividing normal connectivity —
Saves me: those unextinguished fireworks,
Excitement threading me, knotting the fuse,
As dynamite blows everything skywards.

NICK OF TIME

Part I

Chop Suey Looie's Litchi Lounge is shady,
Discouraging reflection while aiding
Conviction as a stiff *Lover's Volcano*
Erupts in my brain. Your excitement shows:
Church bells will chime next week. You'd wanted *me*
There first. I'd never said no to you. We
Were like that: love-opened minds knew no shame.
Untamed, Eden's plants, knowing throbbed in our veins.
But nothing stays the same.

Part II

Matinees — my martinis — agree with me.
Cozy in the Winter Garden, hungry
To sample doctored drama, I see his kid
Brother's chance: stand-in leading man — a bid
For fame. Grease-painted younger, playing to the
Balcony, reflecting on love, making me
Believe. Backstage, uncle shows his set
Of twin photos. Ro, cry-baby, Mommy's pet
With *his* god-child. "Heartbreaker!" he proclaims.
Merry eyes follow till I hear my name.

MEKONG DELTA

They're white as rice that wasn't thrown at us.
His stack of letters (nineteen-sixty-eight's
Mail, barely legible) was saved, penned straight,
Not far from enemy lines. Infamous:
The Mekong Delta, toured by curious
Loved ones, prepared to demonstrate
Our grief, disarm now, do what liberates,
Surrendering to the incongruous.

His presence here seems reconstructed as
Those letters fold my world to paper wings.
Why do brave words demand laments? I meant
To re-read, gather them for warmth — whereas
I light a match, red breast flames releasing
Angels illegible in their ascent.

THUNDER POLKA

The thunder polka of a new romance
Began today on my left foot, the one
Believed to lead suggestiveness astray.

True love's a waltz: it's measured and mature
Like patience set to action. Dance decodes
The blood, translates the shadows of the soul,
Emotions dipping, swelling at the door
Called "sense." Romance corsaged my heart and wrists
Again. Will filled my dance card out because
That blinding barrier shores up dreamwork.

Hopes rubbed together. Sanity, once my
Sly chaperone, no longer is with us.

VESPERTILIO [BAT]

In Mexico, we honeymooned, my first
Time viewing the Pacific. Sunset dressed
A disenchanted evening as we dared
To peer across where barrenness can't be
As bearable as when, relieved by rocks,
Distinctive curving greens, one sure thing there
Reminds us our world hasn't been erased.

The moon stayed in. There's nothing light tonight.

Stiff bristled fear dug tracks in my scalp till
We plug extension cords in lamps, parade
Out on an Acapulco balcony
Like bridesmaids, hoping for some bats, their red
Machinery of appetite alive
This hour, ready to devour my edge
Of desolation. Batwings flap, a sound
Like crisp applause, but, spotting lights below,
Some hide a tiny face in their arms like
Shy children. It's so black, infernal all
Around, when this nocturnal choir rides.

Through wind, they speak to me, the antidote
To barrenness, forever pushing on
Despite the vast uncaring, steadying,
As if wings were things that released my day.

SECRET MIDTOWN GARDEN

Our first apartment bordered ugly Hell's
Kitchen, a place for hanging your head out
The window, yelling for "police, police!"

The back door was my savior, leading me
To jade insertions of a picket fence
That hid a missing piece of Paradise,
Green growing something quite unlike itself.

Here: rose aroma heavy in blue air,
Pink heliotrope lovely as a laugh,
Mature hydrangeas, honey in their cheeks,
Green eyefuls powering up two lives when
The wormy world of midtown leaves the mind
Without its moorings. Secret is our yard,
And lion-lit for us alone, as bold
As some unanswered prayers — survivor's way.

When he complains — "Always outdoors!" he'll say,
"Bent, knees-down!" — I plead debts I owe the day.

EXPECTING BABBO NATALE IN CORTINA

I can't find warmth. It's not our altitude,
The Alps' substantial snow that fashions shapes,
New powder coating life, replenished nights —
When bodies are restored, small tissues knit.

Our private proofs of love, sought after dark,
Materialized, bubbled on bedsprings,
Where we discovered sources: love's issue,
Like riches stored in secret places — we
Becoming multiplied. And we sang praise
To blood that won't remain alone, praised love
That fashioned newborn shapes — maternity,
Till one excluding cry — then silent nights.

I can't get warm since watching that Snow-Cat.

I skied its tracks spooled 'round some evergreens,
And thought of children playing Christmas Day
Around our tree, discarded tissue balled
Near opened presents, newborn joy in place.

That manscape tows me back to bed. You get
Me in a head-lock, then a white tangle.

Outside, there's carolling, their voices raised
To praise one deer. The sauna whistles steam,
As we're replenished red, in sweat, in leaves.

CENTO: NIGHTSONG FOR MOTHER

Mother, dying—mother not wanting to die.
The mother says, I am afraid.
Mother's sitting on the bed with her tattered list of dispersals
— who gets what.
Machine of the mother: white city inside her.

When my mother died, she took home along with her.

Grief has its own gravity.

I rose at the dead of night … to look for my Mother's ghost.
Something is dancing on leafdrift, dancing across the graves.

Line 1: "Mother's Hands Drawing Me" by Jorie Graham, 2016.
Line 2: "Mother and Daughter" by Hayan Charara, 2016.
Line 3: "Mother's Closet" by Maxine Scates, 2005.
Line 4: "Mother and Child" by Louise Glück, 2001.
Line 5: "My Mother Died with Her Home" by Temidayo Jacob, 2019.
Line 6: "Letter to My Mother, One Year after Her Death" by Megan Merchant, 2019.
Line 7: "A Chilly Night" by Christina Rossetti [1830-1894], 1904.
Line 8: "Mother Garden's Round" by Muriel Rukeyser [1913-1980], 1955.

MOTHER ON MORPHINE

A madman crushed her favorite make-up
To paint my mother's floor. Imagine rouge
On top of powders, scattered door to door.
"I'll clean this up!" I say till she's relieved,
Obedient enough to swallow her
Tart, medicated, Lotos-like ice cream.

She's less combative, calmed by her morphine.
The mind's embrasures, freed from pain's embrace,
Will search for entertainment and escape
Confinement, longing to erase what's real.

Mom's traveling through Tinseltown and Rome
Of sixty years ago, a fond time when
Magnani commandeered "The Rose Tattoo."
Perhaps to mother films were fancy cures.

An audience suspected everything,
Eventually, would turn out just fine.

My mopping scrolls sweet fictions she can screen
Through fantasy, delaying hideous
Mortality, the final credits roll,
When shovels dance and dust returns to dust.

Since Roxanol has brought its soft hammer
To bear on mother's habit of rebuke,
We're playing she's an actress, which helps script
Our mock reality. We call this place
"A dressing room," her home "a trailer" parked
Aside the set. She's idle now because
It's needed — her director will demand
That shot where she looks rested. It's agreed
She'll close her eyes while I beat grief from rugs.

Making a comeback, newly patient, she
Rehearses. It's an unfamiliar role,
With gentle words expressed with self-control,
Extending herself to unseen marquees.

Detecting flickers of excitement keyed
By movie light, I hope there's room for me.

AN AMARYLLIS FOR CHRISTMAS

Part 1. During Lent

Resuscitate the wilted, raise what's close
To death: on their lanai I'm still green
At miracles, surrounded by a sky
Gone cold, thin tendrils, others that curled up
In self-protection, living through dying:
My mother's crown-of-thorns, old hens and chicks,
Impatiens, rosary vines, all consigned.

I'm trusted to recover favorites
Forgotten in ruined grass blades wisped away
With those resigned to layered loss by knives —
With dignity. In its own bed, blood-red,
An amaryllis, prized, waits, hibernates.

My mother's eager to succumb to bloom.
She's overdue for majesty, that awe.
O, mater nostra, fiat voluntas tua.

Part 2. Flashback: A Past Christmas Season near Tampa Bay

It's Safety Harbor's Gulf of Mexico
Producing Christmastime's Cancerian
Heat in December that confused this bulb.

Amidst the presents and nativity,
Its empty cradle strewn with straw, green life
Ripped up gay mummy wrapping, and tore loose,
Unhampered by its ground like Lazarus
Unbound. My parents, unprepared for ghosts
Of miracles, became unnerved by sounds
Newborn right by their crèche, the fir tree's base,
Invisible and inexplicable

Like faith. Or like remission. After Mass,
They find a determined amaryllis, force
That sleeps but cannot die, that mother took to heart.

Part 3. During Advent

The screened lanai cured by potent sun
Makes specimens thrive but this takes its time —
Determined amaryllis — teasing us,
As if it knows that mother needs no plant
That grows on mortal soil. Examined, though,
Our last time, blood has rushed, its bud has blushed
A crimson that can only mean one thing.

I rush to mother, "*Vivat!*" in my heart.

The priest has come for her Confession, led
With rosary-wrapped raised hands. "*In vitam
Aeternum*," my lips chant along with theirs,
Head bowed out of respect, my eyes still holding on.

THE GRIM REAPER AS HOUSEGUEST

Amid buffed blackness of the guest room's drapes,
His baritone commanded me to *GO*!
"What's this about?" I want to say. But "No!"
Emerges first. "I'm staying!" There's no cape,
No hood, no scythe. Night hides his shrunken shape,
Revealing just his James Earl Jones audio
Repeating *GO*! Asleep, I'm puzzled, slow
To understand. I rise. There's no escape.

Lost in the territory of morphine,
You turned off your oxygen, approached death's ledge.
Observed by him, I help you breathe again.
His timing's off — though we'll soon reconvene.
A grimace rises from the bedding's edge
As if to say, "Not *now*. I'll tell you when."

THE LAST VISIT

Lined up like make-believe guests, potted ferns
Adorned the entry, their cool shadows dim
Switching the parlor — life's last living room —
Where time hesitates and dark furnishings
Project inarguable dignity.

Bookended by brass casket handles, lids
Too heavy to be raised again must sense
My presence, those defiant eyes I closed,
Who parsed my childish alibis, whose last
Wink nicked the priest, who forced death to hold still
Till her eyes sent light leaping into mine.

Make-up achieved the requisite life-like
Illusion, simulating deepest sleep.

Anxieties from cancer, agony,
Diminishment, decay, helplessness:
These were dissolved by death's majestic wand.

No longer glued in sickbed amber, she
Exhales departure's cloudburst, stretches free,
Ignores those funeral displays. I feel,
Inside pink satin, energy's astir.

Longing embedded in the earth has been
Roused, charmed from sleep to welcome her. Except
Tomorrow's pre-dug grave will not confine
Zest's essence — just her perishable corpse.

Bright windows fogged. Or was that tears? She's flown.

MY MOTHER'S GHOST DANCING

That year morphine became a minuet,
Sweet pianissimo. Its soft pedals stilled
Anguish, reproached relentless timekeeping —
Tick, tick — mortality's metronome.

Before my mother died at home, she learned
That cancer's like a Depression Era
Endurance contest: the dance marathon,
Odds stacked against her, swaying in slow mode.

Despite defiant hair, a plump physique
Deceiving guests, illness hokey-pokeyed
Her organs, shook breasts off, rhumbaed her cells,
Vitality an unremembered song,
Mere noise until sweet exhalations ceased.

Her corpse was wheeled away. The tempo changed.

Dynamic force reclaimed the rooms, infirm
No longer. Energy expressed intent
As if Mom were at a debutante's ball,
Star of the floor show, sequined, applauded.

The mind's embrasures, freed from pain's embrace,
Seek entertainment, longing to erase
What's real. Belonging to another realm —
Where everyone's transparent —Mom's got plans
She's telepathed. But first she wants to dance.

A coldness sidles up to seize my hand.

BIO IN THE SKY

Skywriting life in images, improved
By flourishes, my style is prettified,
That twist on each descendent well-controlled.
(— No one's approaching, Memory. Exhale! —)

Skywriting's all dream-dusted, iced on blue —
Like ghosts no horse will bear. Valves regulate
This airshow billboarding my parents, not
Exposed before like gods. Allowances
Come first. Spray-point my Mom. Come hitch her up
To model height: a famous diva tufted
Ring-tossing love our way, streamed harmony
We might expect to hear near rainbowed curls.

My father's plume-smoked features lit with love
Almost appear as I back up to what
I missed: affection gaining on itself,
Creating the illusion someone's pleased
Possessing me. These masks refuse to hold,
Become safe haze, while shrinking, curved towards earth,
Whose gravity foils some ideas. This realm
Has high rewards yet nothing's closely held.

My smoke-jets off, I fly past our old house,
Gaze through lowered sights. Who loves there now?
Steam wept on panes as darkness skinned green boughs.

CENTO: NEVER-ENDING NIGHTMARES

The dream asks meaning to patch its rags.

Then a nightmare stumbled on my sprawled life.

My nightgown wet with sweat.
I feel you — a sack of scavenged skulls on my chest —
Sipping the salt from my breasts.

Say nightmare, say it loud
At the boundary of madness.

Line 1: "Nightmare, Daymoths" by Anne Stevenson [1933-2020], 1987.
Line 2: "Nightmare" by Frank Chipasula, 1991.
Lines 3-5: "The Nightmare: Oil on Canvas, Henry Fuseli, 1781" by Paul Tran, 2018.
Line 6: "Nightmare Begins Responsibility" by Michael S. Harper, 2000.
Line 7: "The Nightmare" by Hédi Kaddour, 2000.

CEDAR WAXWINGS

My youngest sister's dying first. That's not
How it's supposed to be — thoughts I push hard,
Harder, the small soprano in the swing
Flying to greet the blue with her high C.

She has her mother's eyes, and begs for more
With promises she *will hold on*! — a good girl
Who's never-never-bound. Soon she won't fit
In this contraption, chubby legs too close
Already to the frame. I've just explained:
Some things grow fast like cedars — massing thick
Enough to matter, so strong they repel
Most other forces. High above us now
Cedars shield us from wind, block the cold rooms
Where promise grows, exposing flesh closer
To bones, a chest without hope, a matter
Of time. Trees near this playground stir, newborn.

Swift cedar waxwings bring their young treats, greet
A vast horizon, optimistic might,
As I try pushing so much weight away.

A girl on a swing, returns to me, again, again,
Protected, safe, and saved. Hold on, my love. Hold on!

CUPID MEETS COVID-19

Bodega flowers filled a paper cone.
My sneeze sprayed daisies, almost made them droop.
We laughed at mismatched clothes we chose for our
First date. The diner's kitchen caught fire.
Fleeing, I lost a shoe. You carried me.
Our whimsical romance began mid-air.

Who could predict your moods? Gold jewelry
Appeared for no occasion. I was charmed —
Till birthdays were forgotten, no excuse.

You were capricious, unpredictable —
Like summer with its need to grow hot, wild,
And uncontained, defying ardor's fort
Of solid, safe familiarity.

Your passion made birds croon new love songs.
Amid chaos of King Eros, we wed.

Soon coughing fits would keep me up at night.
Instead of quitting, you became sneaky,
Enjoying this infernal mistress — smoke —
In private, stoked by her distinctive wreath.

Your kisses tasted unfamiliar now
As nicotine's mad cravings took your breath
Until blood lipsticked pillows and bedsheets.

Your forehead radiated August's heat
In March. Pink mucus stained the bathroom floor.

Hot haste fogged windows as our taxi coughed
Its way from icy curbs, your sneeze ploughing
Down the backseat as wheezing shook the wheels.

Across the street, awaiting news, I felt
Lives catching fire. A new enemy,
Capricious as a home invader, would
Gut precious futures, sky-scratch the stars out.

Trash brushed my boots as I watched worriers
Around me crumple coffee cups empty
Of purpose, smother butts, unhitch blue masks,
As, one by one, we left for home alone.

EMBODIMENT

My sister lives forever in six drawers
Where Mom maintains her clothing, worn, outgrown.

Preserved in cameras, she's chambered,
Sealed shut like darkroom prints, unmoving face
Still undeveloped as her unspent youth.

Moored on his island of bad memories,
Her boyfriend, claiming self-defense, wears stripes.

Nighttime she's back, soft stabled in seizures
Of stars or hovering in ghost orb's mist.

A pinch of lonely air lifts blankets, hugs
Half of my bedding. No heat radiates.

The younger person I still am inside
Peers out. Instead of ghost dents on the sheets,
I see her shuffling the deck, smell smoke
From phantom joints, red lipsticked, decayed dreams
Beyond my line of sight, time's taut trapeze.

I yearn to grab her wrist, yank heart and soul
From cold oblivion, yell, "Breathe again!"
Hope hops on life support, prepared to drag
Her from the brink and storm the underworld.

Geometry's shades fade — by dawn's dispersed.

LITTLE TOWEL THIEVES

When had she settled for impermanence
Called other-woman-hood? Affairs had no
Build to them, frail foundations spun thought-sewn
From sugar — a shady borrowed residence.

His wife will never give him a divorce,
Unless the stars align, he likes to say.
Compliance and deceit can't pave love's way.
Contacting Mrs. X was one recourse.

The hope chest she'd inherited (a tableau
Of joyful possibilities) accused
A faith fed by bad intentions. What excused
Her for sustaining a wrongful status quo?

Driving to meet his wife, her prologue spins,
Rehearsing. Shouldn't she apologize?
Some poplars groomed a lesson in disguise:
Like sheltering trees, marriage broke the wind

At a couple's back. Attention cultivates
Roots — not this daze of stolen interludes.
Approaching his house (their home) inner feuds
Pause when she sees a group of children: eight

Sweet little girls in heels played "dressing up."
One swipes white towels from a clothesline. Friends
Affix this bridal veil and Mendelssohn
Her down imaginary aisles, disrupt

Roses — a shower acted out in mime.
The little towel thieves then flee, disperse
Before the laundress sees linen coerced
Into their crime, abandoned, left behind.

Returning home, hands shift into neutral,
Orderly trees receding. Boundaries
Are blurred. Red petals meet the breeze that frees
Them. Night falls on retired rituals.

VALENTINE'S VILLANELLE

Although I've made it holy in my mind —
Our sweet hypnotic love, my fantasy —
That place I left by your side was not mine.

Confounding me with sounds my heart refined,
Unsteady dreaming fanned hyperbole.
(Instead I've made it holy.) In my mind,

Stored, polished memories of us still shine,
Attaching me to what was not to be.
That place I left by your side wasn't mine.

Love's air is thin. Love's words breathe hard, designed
To signify rich unreality —
As though I've made it wholly in my mind.

She drinks you dry, so here you are, inclined
Towards me, embracing chance illegally.
That place I left by your side wasn't mine.

My parents named me for Saint Valentine.
A martyr's passion is his ecstasy.
But though I've made you holy in my mind,
That place I left by your side wasn't mine.

PARTING SHOT

How I wish you were here alone instead
Of with me, poised, on this Italian bridge,
Your fingers fishing for a splashy lure,
Eyes broadcasting to women far and wide,
Undressed lips test-driving warm, speechless lies.

Your hands led me to love's soft alcoves, dear,
As your expression — occupied — checked out,
Consuming many images ahead
Of what developed. Damage lines my life.
My souvenir can't be an exit wound.

Now you're on film, the property of my
New camera, mismatched — mouth still at work
With wanting more, eyes fading while you wave,
Those gestures meeting the indifferent air.

GOLDEN SHOVEL: DEATH CONFESSION

— after Edna St. Vincent Millay

It went awry, our lethal pact — but time
Brings no remorse. Planned suicide. Why does
One die while one survives? Unfairly, not
Unblest, I buried you and mourned yet bring
Dark spectral memories along. Relief
Ends when the noose of night unites dead you
And me. Expelled from light, your ghost haunts all
The same. Clairvoyants say, "Restless souls have
Questions." Confession: feigning death, I lied!

Note: Source poem: "Time does not bring relief (Sonnet II)" by Edna St. Vincent Millay [1892-1950].

Note: First line used: "Time does not bring relief; you all have lied"

THE WAKE

The funeral's assemblage — standing room
Full — humid honeycomb of black-winged veils
Amid a lone queen bee who, rumors say,
Is now quite wealthy, stared as the young priest
Recalled the life of the deceased, a man
He never met. In air arranged by gnats,
This widow might feel the scourge of jealousy
Of wasp-waisted blonde mistresses who sought
The secret bin of sweetness avidly
But dreamt a better end to this affair.

Anonymous bouquets surround his bier.
All roses have been shorn of thorns as if
Transgressive floral displays might cause tears
Throughout the endless swarm from honey-house.

An accidental overdose occurred
Before her husband could file for divorce
As planned. Conspicuously, her eyes close
While mourners pray or check their buzzing phones.

Her mind is cataloguing shameful stings
Of infidelity. Son of a b.

40 DAYS OF WEEPING

Rain poured for forty days and forty nights.
The waters rose until every high hill on the earth was covered.
Everything that lived on land perished in the raging floodwaters
(Genesis 7:21–24)

Raging like rain — the biblical downpour
Impelling Noah to complete his ark —
My tears accumulated, splashed my feet.

While trying to prevent deep sorrow's sea
From drowning me, I ripped up a cargo
Of dry love letters, filling anger's holes,
Till hugs and kisses littered blameless air,
Confessional confetti — meaningless.

Noah invited animals to board
His ark in pairs, the law of two by two.
According to the Book of Genesis,
Nature decreed that to mate is our fate.

Once lovebirds envied us. Now I'm alone,
A star-crossed Juliet, whose balcony
Scene was deleted. Romeo is gone
Along with promised bundles from the stork.

I can't shake off my feelings like breadcrumbs
Consigned to the dustpan. Nightingales lament
Until my pen draws a new pair of wings,
Inky from forty nights' tears. Suddenly,
Comes a new poem — my dove with a branch.

I notice floodwaters are receding.

HERSTORY

The camera lens used to love my face
Until the decades carved away the youth
From my complexion. Everything that cost
Me dearly to acquire — history,
Experience, maturity, kindness,
And patience — crinkled eyes or scarred my skin.

Like an expired passport, an old face
No longer guarantees safe transit nor
Smoothly propels the bearer to love's shores.

Enchant my looking-glass! Reveal real me!

The caustic cackling greets splintered oars.
Night's porters tiredly unlatch the doors.

VISION

The vesper bell solemnifies sunset.
Tomorrow's surgery is on my mind
As steeples come alive, speak to the blind,
Ring out the death of dark itself. Cold sweat
Accompanies my prayers. John Milton's debt
To God was phrased in Sonnet 19, lined
Down by his daughters, to his will resigned.
Should I regain my sight, I won't forget.

But what is 20/20 on a chart
Unless epiphanies root in my heart —
Like music only animals can hear,
Scorched visions that most people could not bear.
Would it behoove me just to stand and wait?
I must spread light before I'm called "the late."

GOLDEN SHOVEL: THE NIGHT'S UNWILLING TO EXPLAIN

— *after Robert Frost*

New York's on fire, crime's dishonest ache. I
Felt displaced, my mouth a gaping prayer. Where have
Benedictions gone? Sainthood's a has-been.

The mayor sleeps with knives. He's not the one
Who'll fix a broken city acquainted
With this blight — where old chime clocks have stopped, with
Questions all suspended. Cops still walk the
Beat but can't protect us. Remember night.

Note: Source poem: "Acquainted with the Night" by Robert Frost [1874-1963], 1928.
Note: Opening line used: "I have been one acquainted with the night."

SERVING ON THE GRAND JURY IN NEW YORK COUNTY

Court officers observe us, single file,
Methodically taking seats without
Discriminating, ten per row with no
Exceptions, hundreds waiting to sit down
In wooden pews, uncomfortable, yet
Designed for cattle calls of young and old.

Blind-folded Justice, symbols of fairness,
American flags decorate this place
Along with foreign faces typical
Of sanctuary cities' melting pot.

I'm confident I won't be picked because
Defense attorneys have rejected me
For years, suspicious of how many books
I've read or something else about my looks.

Some ask to be excused. The clerks asks, "Who
Needs a postponement?" Many hands go up.

Time drags. I'm studying Justitia,
The Roman goddess holding scales. We're taught
These represent her objectivity —
Or equal treatment in a court of law.

Though hungry, I feel no persistent dread
During the rollcall in this vast hall. But
Without a biased lawyer to create
An outcome I expect, my name resounds.

I notice there's an explanation since
Selected jurors are all Caucasian.

We take the stairs avoiding eye contact.

THE SUBWAY PERVERT

Because all dirty crimes we can't unsee
Are kept by brain's biographer, replayed,
The Subway Pervert cannot be erased.

As if by previous arrangement, he'd
Be waiting after class — ten forty-five
PM — his cock unleashed on subway stairs
While masturbating, daring passersby
To stare or stop his public pleasuring.

He blocked the only entrance to my train.

Ignoring him, I'm determined to pass
Untouched. This tollbooth troll outwitted me.
He knew disgust and fear exact their fees.

Women's untold lives are controlled, fish-bowled —
Cat-calling from construction crews, roughed up
By roofies, rubbed the wrong way by frotteurs,
Man-handled by suspicious fiancés —
As hot male breath clouds up once clear water.

I fantasize about invisible
Shields — safe greenhouses with protective glass
For goddesses who'll never be defiled.

NONET: SUBWAY PANHANDLERS

Can panhandlers decode expressions,
My dishonest ache, aware that
Gaps between what five dollars
Buys are something more than
Not enough? The poor
Ride a thin rail
On subways,
Cruel last
Stop.

THE BRIDGE CROSSING

Suicidal dreams suspend questions of the night. Saudi sisters adrift in New York, darkness rowing them to sinister emirates. Penniless. Sorrow transported them to a souk where they barter, trading hunger for another afternoon in America. Fraught memories they finger like worry beads. A close-mouthed sky spits on the indigent. Dirty pigeons point to the river. They've become feathers, light in the arms of kismet.

gold and copper foliage release
the brittle branch with a whispered sigh
floating to meet the earth's
patchwork carpet
their fate fulfilled

Staten Island Ferry. Accusing north winds whip open coats like a Customs Officer. The sixteen-year-old sister imagines gliding through the tide of clasped hands to a safe haven. Liberty's torch reminds the twenty-three-year-old sister of Aladdin's lamp, a jinni armed with wishes. Then a breeze strips a discarded sandwich of its wrapper. Like terns, these two foreigners scavenge for crusts. Ahead seagulls forage for food, squawking rude reminders like impertinent desk clerks.

catching sight
of bleary-eyed reflections
in the hotel's cheval glass
they forgot
the emptiness beneath

Central Park. Facing east, they perform *Salah*. Women walk dogs, shiny dark hair free as a raven's wings, legs bare unlike daughters of their desert homeland, always petitioning men for assent. Decisions will fly tonight, inked on postcards, explaining why return is impossible. Manhattan's mud-tinged sky is brightening to blue. They walk uptown, guided by the path of Bow Bridge as ducks quack complaints. *Still here*?

doves nesting
at the lake's edge
knitting a new home
out of trash
and exhausted leaves

George Washington Bridge. Unadorned steel. A domesticated red lighthouse squats at its base not unlike crusaders' tombs, faithful stone pets guarding the foot. Warm weather wrestles with their heavy coats, rocks buried in pockets. Makeshift shrouds. Winds stir undependable shadows as they ascend, dare nervous legs to reach a high ledge. A dramatic draping is left to the older sibling. Consigning their sisterhood to the pledge of duct-tape, they jump in tandem. Submerged and gone, momentary mermaids, their mighty splash a proclamation.

boats glide over swells
dusk darkening the Hudson River
waves rolling off their backs
late autumn chill gathering power
approaching day of the dead

Note: Saudi sisters Rotana Farea, 23, and Tala Farea, 16, were found on the rocky banks of the Hudson River, duct-taped to each other. Bound together, they had jumped off the George Washington Bridge. Police discovered their bodies on October 24, 2018.

HAZARDS OF NEW FORTUNE

I. Fortune

"Every disadvantage has its advantage."— Ukrainian proverb

"Кожен недолік має свою перевагу."— *Russian translation*

They quit the Ukraine for America, sacred place of new beginnings. Rescuing a forsaken candy shop with workman's grit, the foreigners stretched meager savings like taffy, pining for sweet success. Wrap-around windows shed sunlight on Slavic menus, neatly folded by the oldest daughter. A famous East Village poet dined here often and lured others. Full bellies fast-friended the cash register. Yet manual labor and servility felt lowly as a casual betrayal even as New York repainted their family portrait in greenbacks and gold. At closing time, each customer was tumbled out, like a salt shaker, which magically refilled, then emptied out again. Poised on a chair, the father hung a framed crisp dollar bill next to a crucifix, another object of worship.

daily chores
doubled the weight
born of waiting

II. New

"Flies will not land on a boiling pot." — Ukrainian proverb

"Мухи не сядут на кипящий котел."— Russian translation

New profits parlayed into a real estate portfolio, deeds fingered like dominos. The novice restaurateurs sipped life lazily through a straw of wealth, the holy liturgy of labor now handed off to helpers. After the last patrons left, most of the chairs were up-ended. Across the only round table, the youngest daughter spread a starched lace cloth and the family supped together on smoked kielbasa, fried cabbage, challah bread, boiled potatoes, picking the diced carrots from the borscht to eat one at a time like golden pills — as if to protect themselves from what would come.

polished silverware
family gathers
mouths open as eyes close

III. Of

"The devil always takes back his gifts."— Ukrainian proverb

"Дьявол всегда забирает свои дары." — *Russian translation*

Of a day unlike the rest. Of a sky cutting itself open, bleeding dawn's red fingers down the wall. Of an unbearable pressure. Of air spawning pearls of sweat. Of a terror gliding through squares of daylight on the bedroom floor. Of a father struggling to sit up, watching blankets rise as if winged. Of unanswered prayers to his household saints. Of final utterings unheard from his fifty-year-old mouth. Of wondering why a bedside chair refused to support his weight as a black confusion blotted out morning. Of inner momentum shorted out.

blue-shadowed cue
stilling life's hum
sunshine, trickster, no longer luminous

IV. Hazards

"Fire starts with sparks." — Ukrainian proverb

"Огонь начинается с искр." — *Russian translation*

After the burial, the only son tried on his father's shoes. His real estate inheritance flashed like a radioactive raincoat. Maybe no one else was willing to be Judas, voting for the murder of reasonable stewardship. The dark mountain within beckoned him to climb, to gamble. He graphed his greed on their tenants' gas lines, illegally siphoned from a ground floor café. Inspectors had dismantled unlawful taps and valves, imposed fines. But impatience choked up. Winding his wickedness like a time-bomb, he offered penny-pinching menace to his mother like today's special. Fired up frenzy of milking the portfolio grew hotter until his heart heeded nothing else. One afternoon, sudden sparks shocked the basement boiler, then fireballed, torched two tenements, snuffed out lives. A swift arrest flattened the son's future like a giant's rolling pin, fried his feeble alibi, pulverized his face on the cold docket of public shame. Aware his life wouldn't balance this debt for disgusted jurors, he hailed a taxi to his next hellscape, leaving behind a note for Mama next to an upturned chair. Moments before the rope crunched his windpipe, he looked out a window imagining flames — all those faces waiting to be saved.

red slash
explosion's crescendo —
brick dust pinks pale sidewalks

Note: This East Village (NYC) gas explosion happened on Thursday, March 26, 2015.

THE HALLOWE'EN HOMICIDES, OCTOBER 31, 1981

The crime's forgotten now — except by them.

Interred apart, in graveyards miles away,
They'll rise tonight, October 31st,
To rendezvous in Chelsea, though unseen,
Avoiding doorbells dead ahead, ringing
Assumed to be young trick-or-treaters — not
Gunmen with handcuffs. Even the dark heaved.

Morticians plied cosmetics to disguise
Her ravaged face, a mask Liz kept in place
For their reunion's kiss-fest, lips unused
To parting in delight except for him.

Unlike romantics still alive, spirits
Don't age. Forever 20, Liz shakes free
A brunette waterfall, burrows into
Remorseful Ronald, 39, as if
Love might reverse injustice or despair.

The crime's remained unsolved for more years than
Her lifetime. Nothing new to talk about,
Old topics serve — her choice for grad school, his
Photography exhibits — anything
But shrinking their own hearts into silence,
Adrift in night's black gulf, surrounded by
Costumed ghosts, fake villains, witches masked.

October's dying heat releases the scent
Of souls it's swallowed. Drinking phantom wine,
Canoodling, they enjoy sweet brevities —
Excluded from the bridal carry, joys
Of familyhood, retirement's applause —
Both destined to be destination-less,

Blind shot like pinballs, purely at the whim
Of outside forces, 22nd Street
Drawing them back by some magnetic force
Residing in its lineage of blood.

When crows screech, cutting through pink dawn like knives,
They separate, resume eternal rest,
Its polar loneliness — till next Samhain.

Note: On Saturday, October 31, 1981, photographer Ronald Sisman [February 19, 1942 - October 31, 1981] and his college student girlfriend Elizabeth Platzman [August 4, 1961 - October 31, 1981] were brutally bludgeoned and shot execution style in his duplex on West 22nd Street in Manhattan's Chelsea neighborhood. This crime remains unsolved.

MY DUNGEON GHOST

"If ye will listen to me, but for a little while, I will tell it ... in story stiff and strong..."
— Gawain and the Green Knight

I.

He gave me my first kiss, a kiss which all
Others aspire to be. But that was not
As memorable as when he crept up
Behind me, deep in the stacks with Shakespeare,
And thrust *Le Morte d'Arthur* into my life.

Uther Pendragon, Lady of the Lake,
La Belle Isolde, Lamorak, Galahad,
Gawain and the Green Knight: he'd rattle off
These names like boys on our block recited
Today's New York Yankees' starting line-up.

Under his spell, I became capable
Of sin, adulteress wed to the head
Of Camelot, while disreputably
Cavorting. He cast me as Guinevere,
Himself as Lancelot, my illicit
Paramour. Troubadours lionized my
Beauty. Fortified by my favor, he
Won all tournaments, adoring his new
Heroic entity, the prison-like
Grip of its shallowness, his eyes askew.

Fantasy twitched, hid its murderous heart.

We're library-eyed sixth graders, bewitched
By British poetry, legends, and lore.
He's eleven years old. I'd just turned nine.

Sundays we'd serve God together, speaking
Liturgical Latin, prim altar boy
In the sanctuary, his Juliet
On the balcony — choir loft — voice raised.
"Lead us not into temptation," we'd sing.

In class we'd pass naughty notes, wild words penned
By Malory, Tennyson, and Chaucer.
He dreamt of noble crusades, mighty steeds.
I thought about what constitutes the light
'Round which friends gather, pull each other up.

Three years later, I cast aside wimples,
Tippets, and my power to petition,
As Camelot's queen, for a Papal Bull.

The Round Table was no more, upended.
Graduation. New unknowns descended.

II.

"Sir Knight, if thou cravest battle here, thou shalt not fail for lack of a foe."

There he was on horseback at The Cloisters,
Preparing to joust, taller, brawnier,
More Green Knight than Gawain but, all the same,
A *verray, parfit, gentil knyght.* No words
Passed. *His baner desplayeth, and forth rood.*

When I described his armor to neighbors,
They derided him: college drop-out, drunk,
An unseemly Port Authority cop.

"*Knight or patrolman, he's a barrier
To chaos. Love whatever saves your life!*"
This sassed retort is thought, not said. What nerve.
My words have more heft than gossips deserved.

Instead I kept my fingers on the pulse
Of Chaucer, Tennyson, Malory, Bede,
Chretien de Troyes, and William Langland,
Earned my degrees by forgetting to sleep,
Becoming an anchoress, books knee deep.

III.

"Where shall I seek thee?" quoth Gawain.

Decades passed. When his voice returned, as if
Magnetic force spun a dusty mix-tape
From life's forgotten hits, as if he'd reeled
Me back to the library's Children's Room,
As if he were transmitting from the spheres,
I was too busy to listen at first.

When his voice returned, insistent, troubled,
It took three weeks before his confession
Was complete. His crimes were unspeakable,
Impressed their brutish force across the miles.

During the course of a contract murder,
His cowardice left an infant to starve,
Bawling inside her crib, though her father
Made provisions for her safe retrieval
From this house of carnage. But the killers —
Two men who'd sired children — did not phone.

In air arranged by bees, the final sting
Blitzed: a slow-witted male was convicted,
Stewed behind bars for nine years, innocent,
Incapable of such a heinous crime,
While my friend refused to speak, let it be,
Abused his liberty by offering
Himself as a paid assassin for hire.

Sweet altar boy, who rang the bells during
Lent's *Miserere*, had turned mercenary.

Arrests came ten years later when he was
Outed. His partner, ill now, suddenly
Decided to name the victim's husband
And him, betraying his accomplices.

Hours spent with the venerable Bede
Enlightened us to the ways of the world,
Its fickleness and instability.
We valued courtly love and *curteisie*.
What incited moral degradation?

"Ye gan to grucche me!" was his sore complaint.
Yet he explained how he sought false glory,
A mad pursuit of titles — duke and king —
Jousting in a mirrored colosseum,
Betraying himself, forever in debt.

Consumed by shallowness, pride, and regret,
My friend had declined a coherent eye.

To offer him cash, I phoned the prison.
"He's been gone a month," the chaplain advised.
"When no one claimed him, inmates dug his
grave."

"Prithee grant an inestimable boon,
My queen, whose loyalty's my only hope.
Family hates me but find my daughter.
Say I'm very sorry and I love her."

I thought of what the Green Knight told Gawain:
Kindness, mercy, and what's "less than to blame."
I pledged fealty. Then he said her name.

A knight ther was and that a worthy man,
That fro the tyme that he first bigan
To riden out, he loved chivalrie,
Trouthe and honour, fredom and curteisie.

Notes: Section headings are all from *Gawain and the Green Knight.*
"verray, parfit, ..." Chaucer, *The Canterbury Tales, General Prologue*, line 72
"His baner desplayath..." Chaucer, *The Knight's Tale*, line 966
"A knight ther was ..." Chaucer, *The Canterbury Tales, General Prologue*, lines 43-46
Note: The murders occurred in Florida on November 8, 1983; John Purvis was wrongfully convicted. My friend began serving a life sentence in 1993 and died behind bars in 2004. No one claimed his corpse.

SPELLCASTING ON SAMHAIN

The customary cry,
"Come buy, come buy,"
With its iterated jingle
Of sugar-baited words:...
— *"Goblin Market" by Christina Rossetti, 1862*

"Night-dyed herbs," came the vendor's cry. "Come buy!
Seductive power. Risk-free trial! Please try
My wares on Samhain!" Odd plants caught my eye.

What did I have to lose? "Can you reverse
Ill-omened destiny?" The crone was terse.
"I'll handle all requests. But pay me first."

Showing your photo only made her nod,
Suspending my belief in priests, saints, God.
Entrusted with my prayers, their grace was flawed.

Counting my money like a cold cashier,
The witch's countenance conveyed a sneer.
October's dying heat lured magic near.

Stroking strange herbs with calloused palms, her quotes
Were incantations. Still inchoate, motes
Re-formed as *you* — grime hanging on your coat,

Death's tight grip meeting life's warm open hand
As you restaked your claim, breathed air once banned,
Embraced me tightly. Was this wonderland?

The crone removed herself, deft as a fawn.
Dismayed, when I looked back, you, too, were gone.

CENTO: NEW YORK NIGHT TALK

There came for lack of sleep, a crosspatch, drained look on the old trees.

Before this dawn tomorrow's *Times* will rustle in the gutter,
And the scavengers will gather our discarded days.

And as the images rewound and the face kept talking, the clear night sky filled up with smoke.

Goodnight, sweet dreams. I thought it wonderful, the lecture we didn't hear;
the bus ride among shooting stars.

Promise tomorrow I will be profligate, stepping into the sun like a trophy.

Line 1: "New York in August" by Donald Davie [1922-1995], 1962.

Lines 2-3: "New York" by Israel James Kapstein [1904-1983], 1930.

Line 4: "New York American Spell, 2001 — 1/ omen" by Tom Sleigh, 2003.

Line 5-6: "New York" by William Justema [1904-1987], 1944.

Line 7: "Sleep" by Meghan O'Rourke, 2005.

LA RUE DES REVES [DREAM STREET]

All day I'm puppet-ized, hands sawing air,
Their movements pained and untranslatable,
Till violet tedium of sunset's sky
When gusts of melancholy lid my eyes.

My mind runs tapes of where I'd rather be,
Erases memory's soiled palimpsest.

Clean bedsheets generate sweet luxury,
Unfold enjoyment's possibilities
On home soil, dimming fierce red real-life blooms.
They disappear, these imperfections, leave
No record how they felt, dragged day by day,
Emancipated from tears, grief's spillway.

Embracing sleep — subversive angel — dreams
Are unmarked roads affirming innocence.

I'm walking paths along my heaven's earth
As bedsprings bear the bother, this great weight.

The end

www.ingramcontent.com/pod-product-compliance
Lightning Source LLC
Chambersburg PA
CBHW020014050426
42450CB00005B/472
* 9 7 8 1 9 1 5 0 2 5 7 7 7 *